How Was I Born?

A story in pictures by
Lennart Nilsson

A Merloyd Lawrence Book
DELACORTE PRESS/SEYMOUR LAWRENCE

Published in Sweden under the title *Så blev du till* by
Albert Bonniers Förlag, AB, Stockholm, and in Great Britain
under the title *How you began* by Kestrel Books.

Photographs copyright © 1975 by Lennart Nilsson
Text and editing copyright © 1975 by Jan Cornell and Rune Pettersson
Medical adviser: Professor Axel Ingelman-Sundberg
Drawings pp. 22-23 by Per Birger Lundquist
Design by Per Olov Larsson

English translation copyright © 1975 by Penguin Books Ltd.

English text adviser: Dorothy Dallas

Manufactured in the United States of America

9 8 7 6

Lithographical work: Angsö Lito, AB, Stockholm

ISBN: 0-385-28624-4

Contents

How you were born

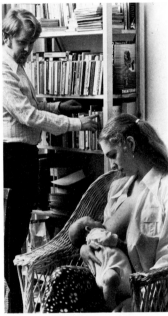

Father, mother and baby right after baby was born.

Babies are hungry and like to get milk from mother's breast. The mother's milk contains everything they need. Babies can live on this milk and nothing else for many months. They can also be fed from a bottle or with a spoon.

Everyone was once a baby and every baby came out of a mother. All children grow; you are growing now, and you will grow for many more years until you are fully grown. Even before you were born, you were growing inside your mother for nine whole months.

The body of every human is made up of millions of tiny parts called cells. Cells which have jobs to do work together in groups, such as the groups of cells which make up your eyes, your ears, your heart.

Once you consisted of only one cell. That cell was an egg cell, about the size of the point of a pin. From this one cell inside your mother, you grew into two cells, then into four, then more and more, getting bigger all the time, until, finally, you grew into millions of cells. Meanwhile, these cells were getting organized into groups, to make your heart, your stomach, your bones, your skin and so on. Because they are organized to do special work, these are called organs.

Inside your mother it was nice and warm, and you were well protected. When you had been growing there for nine months and weighed somewhere between six and nine pounds, you were born and came out of your mother. Do you know how tall you were and how much you weighed when you were born?

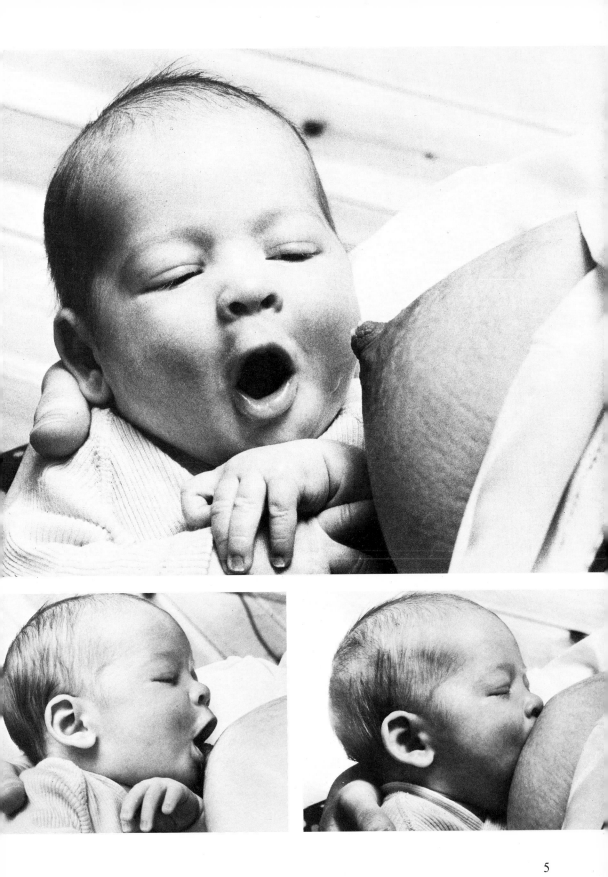

When you had been in your
mother's womb only four weeks
you looked like a little worm.
You can see the head to the
left; the round circle is the
beginning of something that will
become an eye.

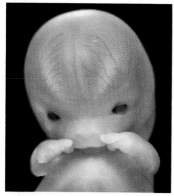

This is the way you looked
from behind when you were a
six-week-old fetus. On top you
see the neck because the head
is bent forward. You can also
clearly see the beginning of
arms and legs.

When you were seven weeks
old in your mother's womb you
had eyes, nose and mouth. But
your fingers were not very
long yet.

As small as
the point of a pin

Inside your mother's belly is a hollow organ
called the womb. You were inside that, in a
"bubble." You were lying in a fluid, called
the amniotic fluid, which is very much like
water. While a baby is there, inside its
mother, it is called a fetus and the "bubble"
is called the amnion. In the pictures you can
see how the fetus lies in the amnion inside
the womb. In the picture on the right the
fetus is seven weeks old. It is turned side-
ways so that you can see the head, arms and
legs. The picture has been enlarged so that
you can see the fetus properly.

Many of the pictures in this book have
been enlarged. Very small fetuses (called
embryos) can be seen only with a microscope.

When you were lying in there, in the
amniotic fluid, you floated around rather
freely. It didn't matter if you were upside
down or right side up then. In the little picture at the top on the left you can see how
funny you looked. At first you were as small
as the point of a pin. Then you grew into
something like a small, crooked worm. When
four weeks had passed your arms and legs
began to show, but you had not grown fingers
and toes yet. After seven weeks you started
looking like a baby, but your head was very
big compared to your body.

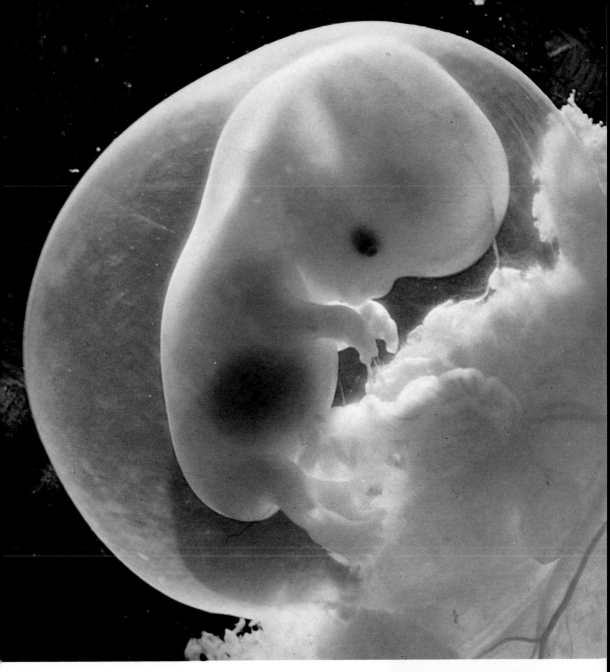

In the enlarged picture above you can see what you looked like when you had been growing for seven weeks. In the beginning the head grows faster than other parts.

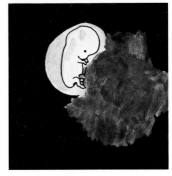

This drawing shows how big you actually were after seven weeks in the womb.

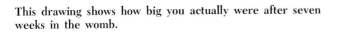

Big head
and small arms
and legs

It was when you were about seven weeks old that your mother became sure that she was going to have a baby. She noticed it in different ways—first, because she did not get her monthly period called menstruation. This is the bleeding a woman has once a month from her vagina, the hole between her legs where the baby will come out. Little girls do not have this bleeding. It starts when a girl is somewhere between eleven and sixteen years old. Other changes began to take place in the mother's body, such as slightly swollen breasts.

Small chubby fingers and a pug nose—that is what all fetuses have after nine weeks inside the mother. They are 4 centimeters (1½ inches) long; the eyes are half-open and the head still bent forward.

A fetus is small and rather transparent. In the pictures below you can see the bones in the hands and feet. You can see the fingernails as well.

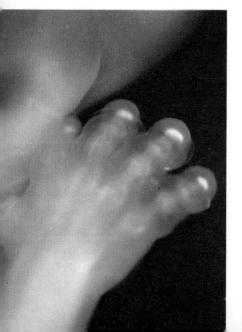
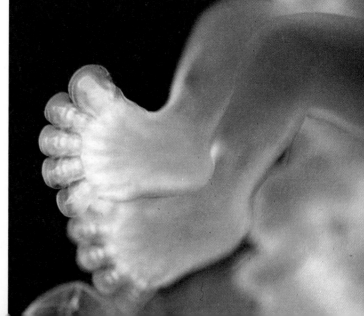

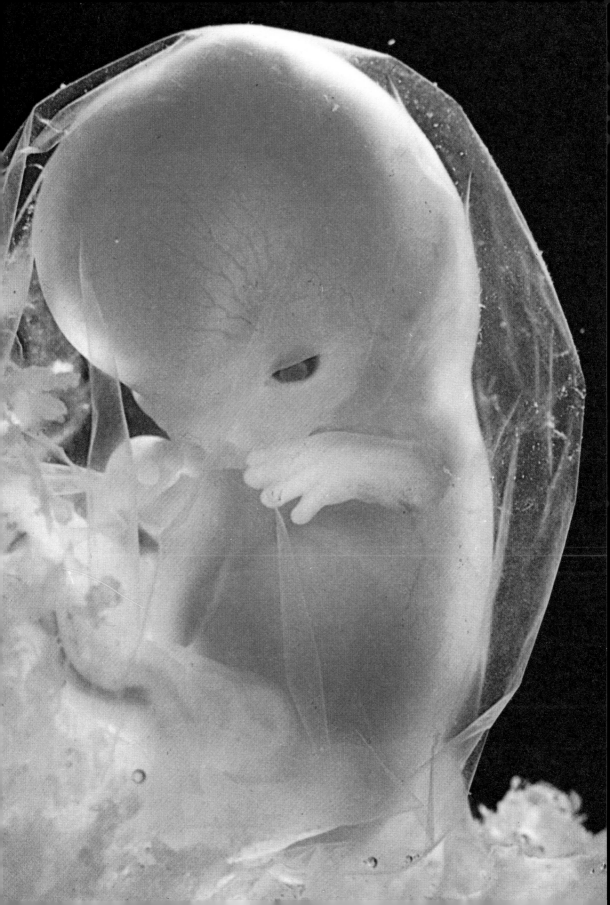

How were you fed in there?

When you eat, you put food into your mouth and after you have chewed and swallowed it, the food goes into your stomach and from there into your intestine. In the intestine the valuable parts of the food, called nourishment, are transferred into the blood. The blood vessels carry it around everywhere in your body. The parts of the food which are of no use to the body go right through you and out of your body when you have a bowel movement. Water and other waste are also carried out as urine.

When you were lying inside your mother, you did not eat with your mouth. Food passed directly from your mother's bloodstream into yours, through a tube called the umbilical cord. This was attached to your belly. The blood vessels running through this cord gave you all the nourishment you needed to live and grow. The other end of the cord joined the womb where the wall was especially thick. This thick part is called the placenta. In the placenta the blood vessels of the mother and the fetus lie very close and here nourishment and oxygen pass from the blood of the mother to that of the fetus. Any waste in the baby's body passes back into the mother's blood. She gets rid of it in her urine or even in the air she breathes out.

In the center of this picture you can see the umbilical cord and the blood vessels inside it. The cord goes from the belly of the fetus through the amnion into the placenta. There the big blood vessels separate into many small vessels that lie very close to the small blood vessels of the mother.

When you were born the doctor cut your cord. It healed quickly and what is left now is the small dent called the navel, or "belly button."

This is what a fetus looks like when it is nine weeks old. The neck is still as thick as the head. The arms and legs are still very short.

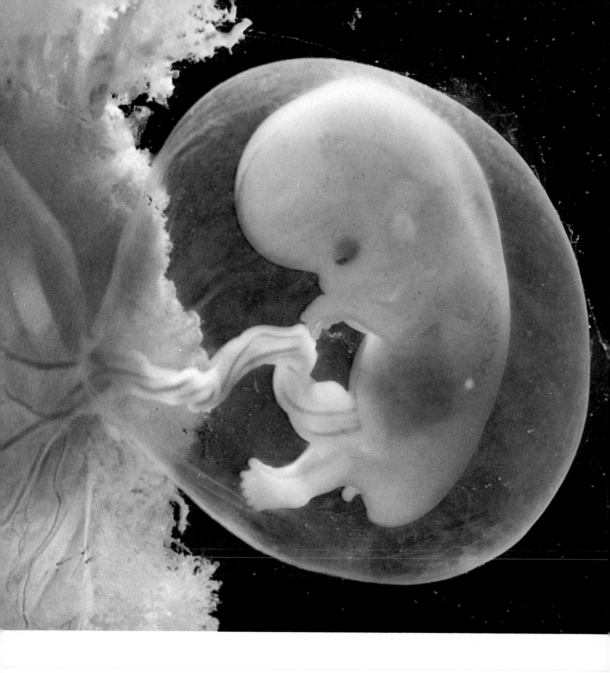

The tail and other odd things

Before we were born, for a short time, both you and I had a tail. A five-week-old fetus has a tail. In the big picture you can see what you looked like when you had been in the womb for about five weeks. The tail is curved: the pointed part shows between the short legs. You were very small then, about one half inch long. When you went on growing, the tail disappeared.

A little human fetus looks like the fetus of lots of other animals. For instance, during the sixth week there were small slits on your neck. A fish fetus also has these slits. When the fish grows, these slits become gills and the fish breathes with them under water. The gills take oxygen out of the water. But in the human fetus the slits disappear for they are not needed:

Human beings and animals are alike in other ways, as you know. We have eyes, nose, stomach and legs and so do many animals. In the very beginning, the bodies of humans and animals start growing in just about the same way. But soon each different type of animal develops in its own particular way. As early as seven weeks, the human fetus is clearly human.

In the picture on the right you can see the curved and pointed tail sticking up between the legs, which look like little paddles.

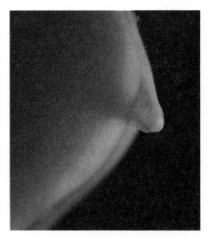

The tail is much smaller when the fetus is three months old.

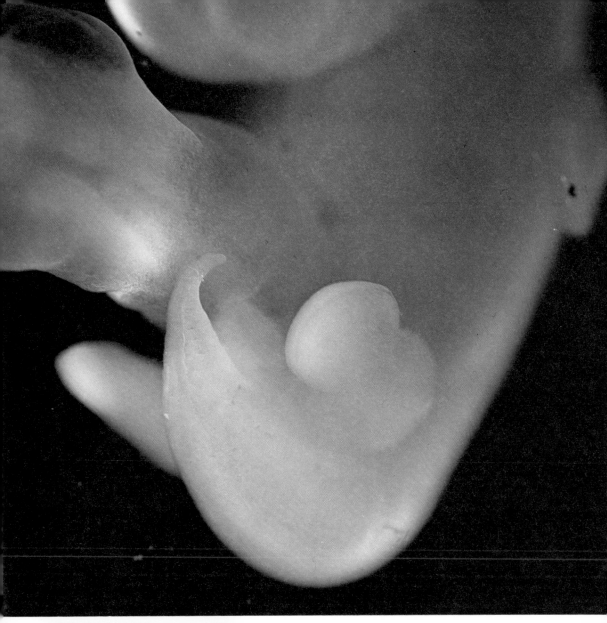

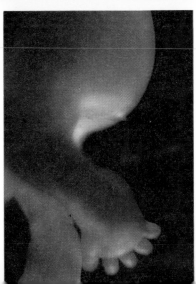

After about four months the tail has almost disappeared. There is just a tiny knob left and by the time the baby is born that too has disappeared.

The fourth and fifth months

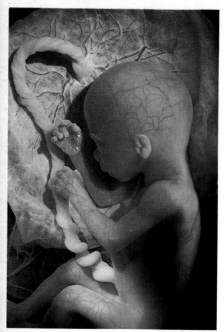

This is what you looked like after four months in the womb. You can see the cord clearly. The arms are longer than before and there is a proper neck. The ears are not quite completed yet. At this age you were about 16 centimeters (6½ inches) long and you weighed not quite half a pound.

During the first few months the fetus is so small that it floats. But in the fourth and fifth months the fetus begins to bump against the walls of the womb. When it kicks and starts, the mother can feel it moving—as if something were fluttering in there. This is very exciting to the mother. Doctors call it the "quickening." Later, near the time of birth, the baby is bigger and stronger and can push hard against the walls of the womb. Then the mother and father can watch as the baby kicks. They can see its feet making the mother's belly bulge here and there.

The more you grew inside her womb, the more your mother's belly grew. When you were five months old, it began to be quite round. Anyone putting an ear close to her belly could hear you moving around in there, and when the doctor checked up on your mother's health he also listened through his stethoscope to hear your heart beating.

After the fourth month in the womb, your face was well organized with forehead, eyebrows, eyes, mouth and so on. At this stage your eyes were closed while they grew. Your hands also nearly reached their final shape during this month. In the photo to the right, you can see the fetus in the transparent bag called the amnion. The amnion cushions the fetus in a pool of fluid. You may wonder why it doesn't drown. This is because a fetus doesn't breathe. It gets all the oxygen it needs through the cord from its mother, just the way it gets its nourishment. You did not use your lungs at all until after you were born.

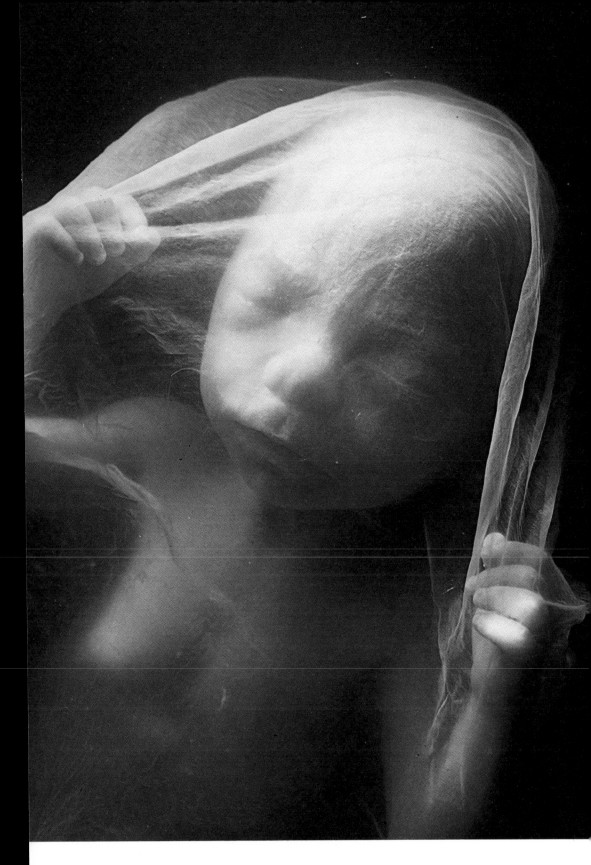

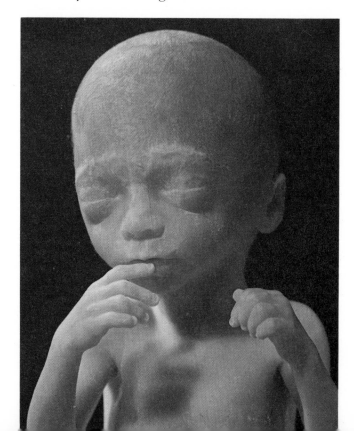

The last few months in the womb

At this stage you were growing in just about the same way that you and other children grow every day. You became taller and heavier, but your looks did not change. Mostly you slept. But some of the time you were awake and moving your arms and legs. Sometimes a loud noise startled you, because you could hear quite well. If your mother moved unexpectedly, you gave a start and kicked!

Hair grew all over your body, like a monkey. Some babies are born with soft hair on their ears and foreheads, but most babies lose this extra hair before they are born. What happens to the skin on your fingers when you hold them in water too long? It gets crinkly. This did not happen to your skin when you lay in the fluid, because it was protected by a kind of grease.

In the last couple of months the fetus has to lie tightly curled up. But when you were as small as this, none of the bones in your body were very long or very hard so it did not hurt you.

In this picture you can see the protective grease, especially on the lips and eyebrows. This is what a fetus looks like when it is six months old.

16

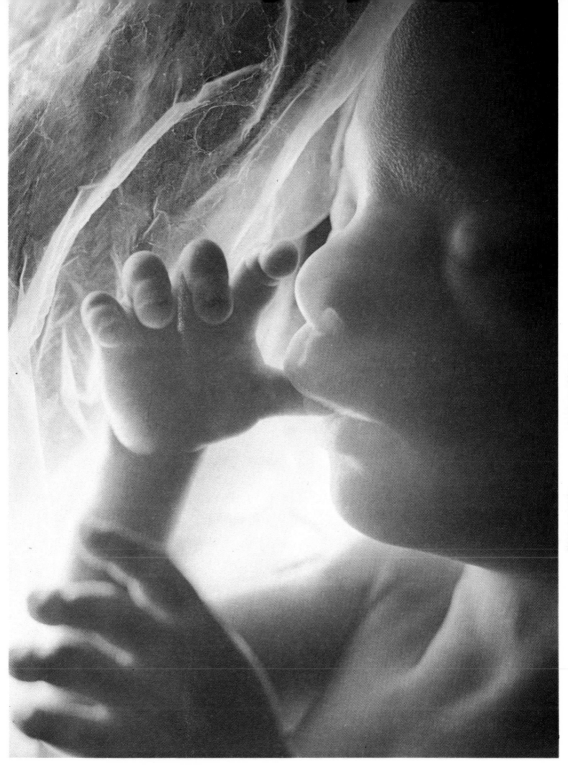

When you were four-and-a-half months old you began
behaving like a newborn baby. Sometimes you had your
thumb in your mouth. You did this as a kind of practice, so
that you would be ready to suck at your mother's breast.

Your birthday

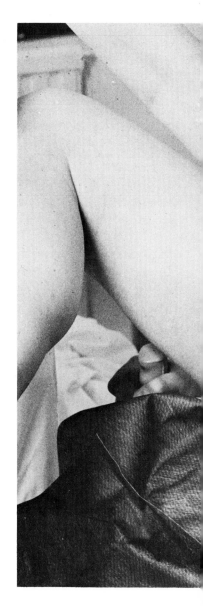

You came out of your mother's body through the hole between her legs called the vagina. This hole stretches easily to let the baby through. Afterwards the hole becomes narrow again. At the time of birth, the womb begins to squeeze and let go, squeeze and let go, and the baby is pushed out. The squeezes are called contractions because the strong muscles of the womb get shorter when they are giving the baby a squeeze. Giving birth is very hard work for a mother. Afterwards she has a great feeling of relief and joy.

In the picture you can see how the baby is coming out. The doctor and nurses stand by to help the mother and receive the baby. The baby is usually born head first. After the baby has come out, the placenta follows. The doctor makes sure that the baby has started to breathe properly and he cuts the umbilical cord.

The day you were born you were given a bath. Then you were weighed on the scales and measured. Soon after birth, babies are given their mother's breast where they suck the milk they need to grow on. If there is not enough milk in her breasts, the mother (or father) can feed the baby from a bottle with a nipple.

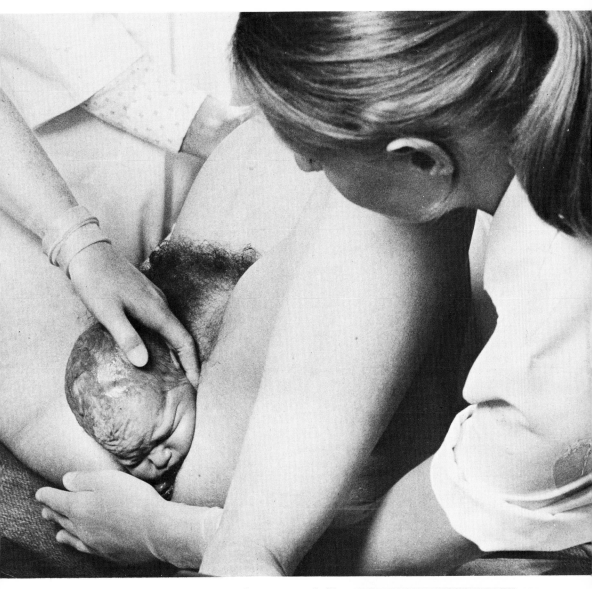

One minute after you were born you probably
looked as tired as this baby. Birth is hard
work for the baby as well as the mother.

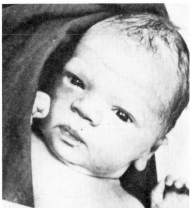

Here are three girls and a grown woman. The girls are 8, 14 and 4 years old. The woman is 24. When girls are 10 to 14 years old their breasts begin to grow and they begin to get pubic hair at about the same time.

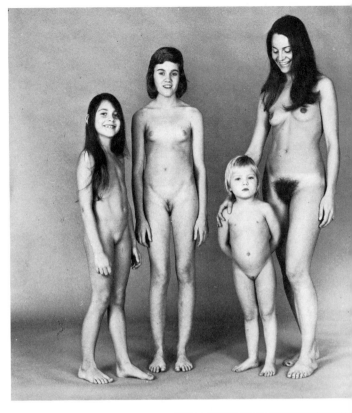

When boys grow into men they become stronger and have bigger muscles. The man here is 23 years old, the boys are 4, 16 and 10. Most boys' penises are fully grown by the time they are 16 and most boys have deeper voices by then. Different boys have different size penises but that is not important. Boys grow hair around their penises, under their arms, and on their faces. The hair around the penis, called pubic hair, is fully grown by the time boys are 18, and their beards about two years later.

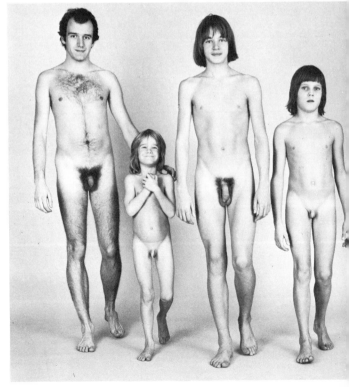

How did you get in?

You came out of your mother on your birthday. For nine months you had been in there, growing from one cell, as small as the point of a pin, into millions of cells—into a baby. But how did you get in there in the first place?

The tiny egg from which you grew was made in your mother's body. This little egg cannot become a baby by itself. Another sort of cell called a sperm must be joined with it. The sperm is made in the father's body. It is too small for you to see except with a microscope. The egg is the size of the tiniest dot you can make with a pencil. It comes from the mother's ovaries. She has two ovaries which are exactly alike. They are placed on each side and a little above the womb, one on the right and one on the left.

Sperm cells are produced in thousands in a grown man's testicles, which are in a pouch of skin under his penis. The sperm cells are carried through a tube up into his body and then out through another tube, called the urethra, where his urine goes.

This is a drawing of a grown woman. The green parts show where the genital organs are. (These are the parts of the body which help to make a baby.) At the top, to the right and left, are the ovaries. Two tubes, called the Fallopian tubes, begin next to the ovaries and end in the womb. The bottom of the womb opens into the vagina.

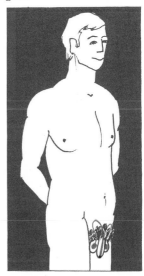

This is a drawing of a grown man. The red parts show where his genital organs are. The testes lie in the pouch (or scrotum) behind the penis. Here the tubes that carry the sperm begin, and they empty through the penis, along the same channel by which the urine leaves the body.

How are children made?

When a mother and a father want to start a baby they begin by lying beside each other, naked, and hugging and kissing. The father's penis becomes hard when they lie like this

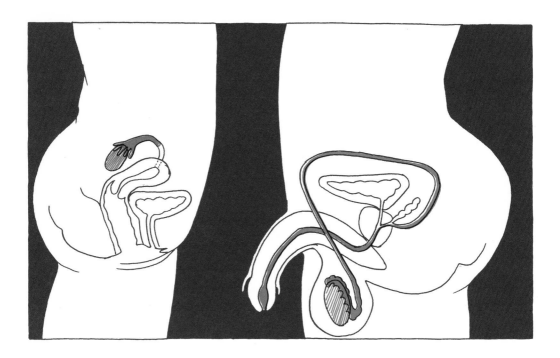

and he puts it into the opening between the mother's legs, the vagina. This is the same opening out of which the baby will one day be born. The vagina is like a tube that leads to the womb. While they are doing this they feel loving and very good all over. This is called sexual intercourse.

After a time the sperm cells jet out of the father's penis into the mother's vagina. When the sperm are in the vagina they begin the long swim up into the womb, and then from the womb into the tubes, called the Fallopian tubes, which lead the eggs down from the ovaries. In one of these tubes a sperm cell meets an egg cell and joins with it—when that happens a baby is started. This is called conception, which means beginning.

The penis is made so that it can stand up and become hard and go into the vagina easily. There are spaces inside it which can fill with blood and so make it stand up, like a rubber glove when you fill it with water. A man's or boy's penis can become hard even if he is not lying next to a woman. And a man

On the left above is a woman. The large tube leading out of her body is the vagina. In front of it is the bladder and from this another tube carries her urine out of her body. At the top of the vagina is the womb and over that is one of the ovaries. The green color shows the way the egg travels, from the ovary into the Fallopian tube.

On the right is a man. The urine is collected in his bladder and goes from there through a tube in the penis. Behind the bladder there are two bags containing the fluid where the sperm live. You can see only one of the bags in the picture. The sperm are formed in the testes. The red color shows the way the sperm travel, from the scrotum through a tube which leads into the urine tube, through the penis and out of the body.

22

and woman can lie together and enjoy hugging and feeling the penis slide into the vagina without wanting to start a baby.

In each of the ovaries there are thousands of egg cells. Once a month one of the ovaries lets an egg cell go. In the tube the egg travels towards the womb. The egg cell travels very slowly. If it gets fertilized by a sperm cell, it clings to the wall of the womb and starts growing. The lining of the womb is prepared for the egg with a soft lining of delicate blood vessels. If no fertilized egg reaches the womb, the lining is shed once a month. It flows through the vagina like blood. This is called menstruation, or the monthly period. Menstruation begins to happen once a month when a girl is between eleven and sixteen years old.

The drawing on this page shows what happens when the mother and father have sexual intercourse. The penis is inside the vagina. The red color shows the long way the sperm have to travel from the scrotum to the Fallopian tube. At the end of intercourse the sperm tubes and the sperm bags contract so the sperm are pressed out of the penis and into the vagina. There they start swimming under their own power through the womb and into the Fallopian tubes. Only one of the many sperm can fertilize an egg. The egg's way from an ovary to the Fallopian tube is marked in green. The fertilized egg is then carried into the womb where it develops into a baby.

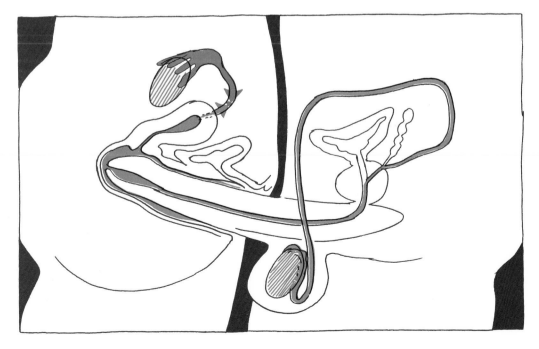

The long journey of the sperm to the egg

The sperm swim hard toward the egg. The sperm is a cell with a head, and a tail which it wiggles in order to swim through the fluid in which it lives. Both sperm and eggs live in fluid. They cannot live in the air because they would dry up. You can see the egg in the picture on the right. This egg is photographed in the Fallopian tube as it is slowly carried down towards the womb. The white dots around it are the sperm.

The egg on the right is much enlarged. In reality it is not bigger than a pencil dot.

Sperm on their way to the egg. This picture is very much enlarged so that the sperm can be seen.

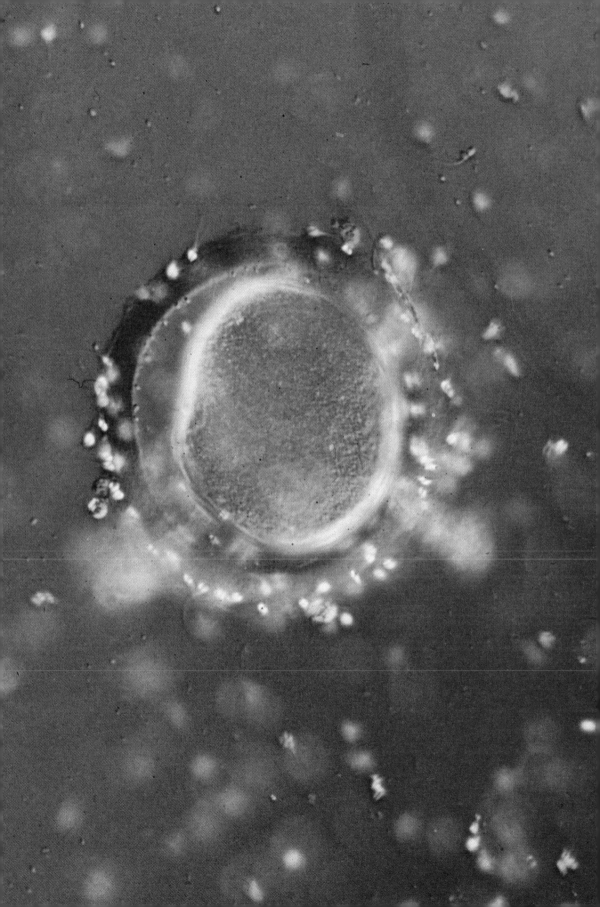

The moment
you were conceived

On the left you can see some sperm which have finally reached the egg after their long journey. For such a small cell it really is a long way to travel. Two sperm have reached the egg almost at the same time. When one sperm has pushed its way into the egg, the egg is fertilized. As soon as this happens the

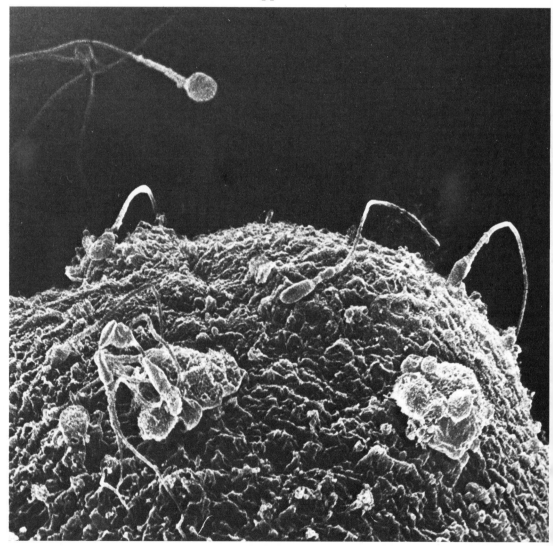

wall of the egg becomes hard and will not let
another sperm in.

In the right-hand photograph you can see
how a sperm has reached the wall of an egg
and is on its way in. When the sperm has
forced itself into the egg, the two join and
become a new and bigger cell which is called
a fertilized egg cell. This cell starts dividing,
and that is how the baby grows. At the very
moment the egg becomes fertilized, a new
human being is on its way.

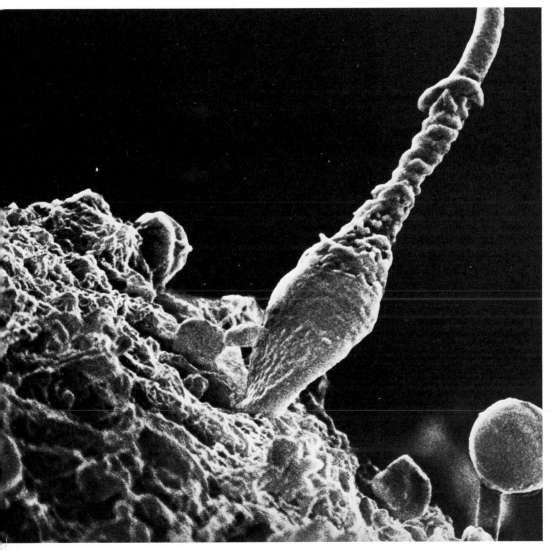

Beginning to grow

A fertilized egg divides itself into two cells. These two cells divide themselves in two and become four. The four become eight, the eight become sixteen and so on. More and more cells develop. The first division happens only a few hours after fertilization. At first the cells look like a lump. But they soon form themselves into something like a hollow ball. One side becomes dented as if the ball has been squeezed. Then the dented ball folds itself and becomes a tube and soon the embryo starts to look like a baby.

In these photographs you can see the cells increasing. On the right is the tiny tube-shaped fetus after about four weeks. The parts which one day will be the head and arms are beginning to stick out of the tube. And so the fetus goes on growing and growing, as you already know from reading the beginning of this book.

Here you can see the egg dividing. One cell becomes two, then four.

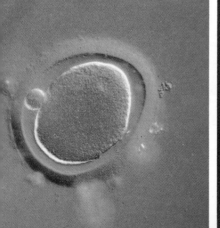
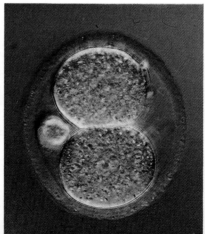

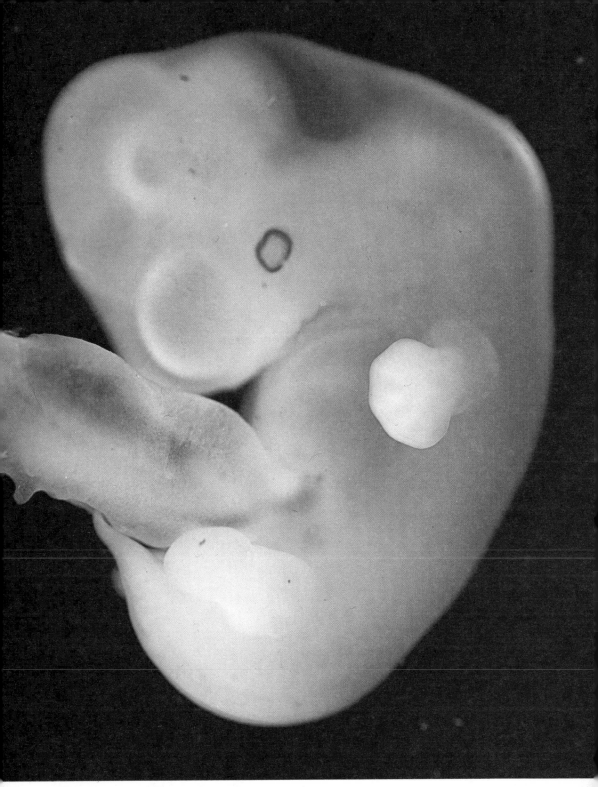

In this picture you can see what you looked like when you were four weeks old. The little circle above the middle in the picture is the beginning of an eye. To the right is the beginning of a hand. The fetus ends in a pointed tail. As you know, it disappears later. To the left you can see the cord.

29

When you came into the world

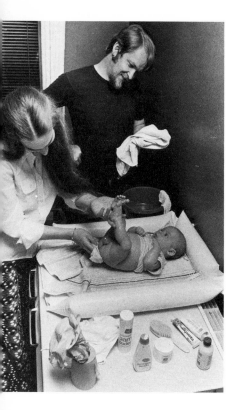

When you came into the world your mother and your father looked after you. Newborn babies cannot look after themselves at all. Only the young of very simple animals like flies or frogs can do that. A kitten or calf has to have milk from its mother so that it can live.

You have probably heard someone say that you look like your mother or your father. Or perhaps someone else in the family. Children often resemble other relatives, because many characteristics are inherited. The color of your hair, for instance, is inherited. These characteristics are carried by something inside the cell called genes. Half of the genes come from the mother and half from the father. They, in turn, received their genes from their parents who got them from theirs and so on back in time. The genes are mixed as they always come from two parents at a time, and no human being in the world is quite like any other.

When you were small you needed someone to take care of you and give you food or help. As you grew older you gradually learned to look after yourself and when you finally grow up, you will probably have children of your own to care for.

Mother and father help each other to tend their baby.